I0163963

Lario Sinigaglia

LANGUAGE:

A DIFFERENT USE OF THE BRAIN

Youcanprint

Title | Language: a different use of the brain
Author | Ilario Sinigaglia
ISBN | 978-88-31631-82-2

Youcanprint
Via Marco Biagi 6, 73100 Lecce
www.youcanprint.it
info@youcanprint.it

INDICE

PREFACE

The main purpose of this essay is to show that natural language, when contextualised, by its nature avoids the paradoxes and the shortcomings ascribed to it.

Preliminarily, I would like to put forward some hypotheses on the origin of language based on hypotheses inferred, in my opinion, in the writings of the American linguist, Noam Chomsky, and the American philosopher, Jerry Fodor.

I also propose a simple, naturalist hypothesis on the origin of natural numbers and therefore of arithmetic. Only chapter 8, on set theory, requires some prior knowledge that the reader of goodwill can easily find even in my previous writings which are cited. Chapter 7 dealing with linguistic paradoxes is complex when addressing the difference between *concepts* and *properties* and requires some engagement by the reader. My advice is to proceed even if not everything is clear in the first reading. You can reflect and take a second look. Here and elsewhere, we do not understand everything right away. Anyone who wants to understand everything before proceeding, should simply not proceed. Proceed, therefore, and you will understand, if not everything, certainly more. Any text that has been important to me has taken time and several readings. I hope that my writing is worth the effort of the reader.

Lario Sinigaglia

1) EDUCATION

A small child of a few years speaks, at ten they write correctly, and at 14 they can be held criminally liable and therefore are expected to know the rules of civilised life. These are the results of a thorough education provided in a civil context. But how did this all begin?

Darwinian evolution follows Homo sapiens back to about 200,000 years ago and, since we are also Homo sapiens, he could have been our grandfather who, even though he did not speak, did not write, nor use utensils and was therefore certainly much smarter than our actual grandfather in managing with his bare hands in an unimaginably hostile environment.

According to Noam Chomsky (1928), the great scholar of language, *Homo sapiens* began to speak quite suddenly around 60,000 years ago and he bases this hypothesis on the emergence at that time of archaeological finds that demonstrate the ability to symbolise the circumstances of human life, relatively complex societies, as well as the population's greater dynamism for growth and migration (Noam Chomsky and James McGilvray, *The Science of Language. Interviews with James McGilvray*, 2012, Italian translation published by Il Saggiatore, Milan 2015).

We therefore follow Chomsky as much for the depth of his studies on language as for the implicit assumption that the linguistic path is the most important one for understanding humans: after all, it is the only characteristic that separates them from the universe of other living beings.

Chomsky admits, however, that the conquest of language was preceded by brain activity which he characterised as *Merge* (to merge:

to add, incorporate, blend together), which is preliminary to the typical compositionality of language.

All these are of course the famous professor's hypotheses and we should abound in the use of the conditional to put them forward (as Chomsky himself does: *it would have been preceded... etc.*). But I like the professor's hypotheses and I will therefore use the indicative, reserving the conditional for my own hypotheses.

But what does the brain *merge* and incorporate? Certainly not words, which do not exist, nor simply images, as every higher animal has certainly done for a long time.

Perhaps it merges "experiences".

Let us return briefly to the present since it remains the best way to explain a past that basically never dies.

Experiences are generally considered a value, but, as we shall see, they have an ambiguous value because you pay for them with the painful currency of mistakes.

It is impossible to gain experiences without making mistakes and we gain experiences only by surviving mistakes.

Training and contraptions of experience simulators can be used but, ultimately, reality is different.

Different from what? From what we thought it was according to information at our disposal.

Let's go back to 200,000 years ago: *Homo sapiens* actually knew next to nothing of what we learn in school today. But, if they managed to survive until then, it is because there was a valid and innate instinctual heritage that was all that they had.

Therefore, to gain experience (since today we gain experience, in the beginning they did the same), *to gain experience*, one must, at least in part, falsify one's own instinctual heritage. That is, behave differently from how instinct tells us to, for example handling fire.

2) EXIT FROM THE GARDEN OF EDEN

Chomsky argued fiercely that the sudden appearance of language is not the result of a gradual, Darwinian genetic evolution. He instead believes that organs (not just the brain) used before, and in a certain way for a very long time, were suddenly converted to other uses.

Just like an instinctual brain that converts itself at least in part – i.e. it splits – and starts to work against itself by diverting and even blocking ancient impulses.

Let us pause for a moment and come back to today. Is this not what we feel happening in us even now?

Is it not true that education has an informative content but more fundamentally a compulsory content to be internalised in order to act even when it is not the educator's responsibility? In fact, the biblical Decalogue is largely constituted by prohibitions.

Let's go back to Homo sapiens: what happened with him?

The Bible is very clear: the Devil misled Eve, who then persuaded Adam. There are reasons to believe that it was Adam who was particularly misled because he was more expendable since he had fewer genetic obligations, while Eve kept most of her instinctual heritage.

In addition to the Devil's persuasion, we can take into consideration:

a) Exceptional circumstances: for example, in imminent life or death danger, *Homo sapiens* holds a firebrand and discovers the advantages of this non-instinctive behaviour.

But we can also think of dysfunctions that prove functional. After all, Darwin has shown that genetic errors can be advantageous. For example:

b) Some *Homo sapiens* go crazy, act against their normal instinct, obtain advantages and they or their companions remember them. After all, in primitive communities, madmen enjoyed special consideration.

c) Some brains of *Homo sapiens* lose synchronisation between the two cerebral hemispheres (due, for example, to an inefficient connection) and these latter acquire mutual independence.

The hypothesis in c) attracts me because I feel it is compatible with what is happening with us even now: we feel unclear inner conflicts; we have dreams that we do not understand; we have illuminations and we experience fascinations that surprise us.

However, *Homo sapiens* had to remember these behaviours against their instincts and their outcomes, which began to become explicit knowledge that was different from what was implicit in their instincts and so they began to emerge from the eternal present that previously absorbed them.

This was, in our opinion, the object being *merged* and incorporated mentioned by Chomsky which was preliminary to language. But with time, a long time by our standards but very little compared to the time needed for genetic evolution, the object being *merged* − those experiences to remember, organise and communicate − required a suitable container and this became language.

3) THE INVENTION OF LANGUAGE

In this perspective, language was a human invention desired and obtained from a brain that no longer served for instinctual responses but also for encouraging behaviours that proved to be effective as a result of experiences that had put instinctual heritage into question. But something new emerges at this point that attempts to coordinate two different strategies shared by the same acting body: much later, this was called the *Mind*.

Chomsky's *Merge* (for us, the sequence of experiences) and language are incompatible with Darwinian evolution due to the short time in which it happened, according to the professor.

The American philosopher, Jerry Fodor, thinks the same thing for a different and well-argued reason: Darwinian evolution requires a basis that can be developed gradually giving progressively higher benefits to the bearer. Language, and its underlying cognitive apparatus, cannot be this basis because it cannot be realised progressively: it exists complete, and therefore it works, or it simply does not exist.

(J. Fodor, *The Mind Doesn't Work That Way*, published in Italian by Laterza, Bari, 2001: contains a series of lectures held by Fodor at the San Raffaele University Hospital in Milan and *Mente e linguaggio*, Laterza, Bari, 2001: contains translations of some of Fodor's essays, with an introduction and translation by Professor Francesco Ferretti)

But what constitutes the completeness of language? There must be:

a) Subject (who, what);
b) Predicate (what it does/is);
c) Temporal measurement (when);
d) Negation (rejection of the status quo).

It should also be noted that there is something found in language, which existed before language but is still found in its expression: a subject that comes from an instinctual *continuum* and thus from an eternal present, which takes action to achieve a change of the status quo. It is also possible to consider counterfactuality and therefore the future. When there is a future, there will begin to be a past. To have also a *history,* writing had to be invented: this happened in the Third Millennium BC.

Therefore, language is only secondarily a means of communication: first of all, it is the individual who lives in a new dimension and has fled from the Garden of Eden striking down the Angel who wanted to keep him there with a flaming sword.

Was this divine or diabolical persuasion? The Bible has no doubts: it was diabolical. While respecting the views of that authoritative text, I think it is still too early to decide.

4) CHARACTERISTICS OF LANGUAGE

In this perspective, language is not only a means to achieve something, communication, but it is the container of the subject's experience, since the subject exists, language and subject are therefore indistinguishable and thus language has a primary and indelible personal dimension.

It is also true that language is a way of exchanging meanings, but this is possible only if the subjects have had common experiences, the first of which is to be raised in the same language area.

But just as experiences are common only up to a certain point, language communicates only up to a certain point, fairly modestly in fact, and only a particular communicator, an artist for example, can go beyond that point.

Behaviours in communities seem harmonised, "as if there were communication", but, in fact, for the most part, it is a convention of many names: customs, manners, ways of the world, traditions, compliance with rules and so on.

We must reflect on the nature of experiences: each experience is a modification of an existing heritage of beliefs and these are only partially explicit. Of these there is awareness: this is precisely the part that is already formed as experience and which is then modified by a subsequent experience.

But one part of our beliefs is implicit and of these, one part is instinctual, presumably transmitted genetically, and another part was unknowingly absorbed by the subject in the early years of life getting an education and, most of all, a particular language that is, itself, a container of beliefs which is very difficult to change as a result of an experience.

In fact, the nature of an experience is to reshape an individual's beliefs, but there are foundational beliefs whose elimination involves almost the very elimination of the subject. This was the dream of every totalitarian regime whose utopian nature we must not hide: to create "the new man".

Sometimes people fail to meet their basic needs, certainly they never manage to achieve their utopias and this seems to me to be evidence of the existence of an order.

Genes could make a new man, but for about 200,000 years now they haven't tried. It is not unusual: crocodiles have had a much longer lasting genetic confirmation: 100 million years.

Each of us embodies in every present the history of our experiences and, if it were possible to make an existential section of us, we would find growth rings similar to those we find after sawing a tree and, just like those, they become closer and closer to one other, because with the passage of time it is increasingly difficult to gain new experiences.

Experiences, in fact, act against themselves: past experiences obstruct future experiences.

This suggests the idea that the process has a direction and it is not simply modelling clay which can be indefinitely remodelled.

During the ongoing succession of experiences, original instinctual heritage is reduced, opening two new dimensions: the future, which is especially engaged in the first part of life (plan) and the past, which is engaged in old age (memory and regret).

With the abandonment of instinctual heritage, there is at the same time an underestimation and an abandonment of the present, which fills our childhood with treasures: glittering stones, tadpoles in puddles, fireflies of the night, and water lilies in ponds.

When an old person is sent into retirement, he no long finds the plenitude that was the present, unless he has been able not to ward it off himself.

The succession of experiences therefore has a sense, the thinning and neutralisation of instinctual heritage that is common to all, though different in each person and this is what we feel as a "passage of time". We then agreed to anchor the passage of time to cyclical phenomena (hours marked by clocks, days and years marked by the sun) but the years that become shorter, like tree rings become thinner, avert us that the experiences are less frequent and that we are ageing.

The "passage of time" depends on experiences and these depend on the mistakes that cannot be predicted and therefore are not included in the future that language has, which is only that of clocks.

So, our real "passage of time", which is what we will be downstream of our experiences, is precluded and our plans do not take it into account: this is what young people do not know and what they, just like us, will learn too late.

I ask the reader to allow me a digression: classical Greek tragedy shows the astonishing dynamic of experience in an unsurpassable way, although few experiences are as tragic as those of Oedipus.

The god of tragedy is Dionysus and Greeks liked to represent him with a cloak hanging in the house: he is there, but not seen until the moment he bursts onto the scene and exacts the cost, never small, for the experience.

In Greek theatre the true target of the experience would have been the spectator and maybe some of them, after the performance, having understood the warning, would hang the god's cloak in their house.

5) THE FUNCTION OF NATURAL LANGUAGE

At any time, a person has certain beliefs resulting from their experiences. Since an experience consists of the falsification of a belief (the earlier truth is now false), those beliefs retain falsified beliefs as memory. That is to say: in the present, a person thinks that what he or she previously believed true is false but he or she doesn't believe anything to be true and false at the same time.

A logician would say that this person adheres to the "principle of non-contradiction".

How does this revision process of beliefs occur? It is not a process but an instantaneous restructuring, which may be local or widespread, of the state of our beliefs. I think that this happens in our sleep so that we are not faced with discontinuity in the middle of an action and that dreams are a symptom of this.

It is said that the night brings counsel and it is true that the new day brings a new way of seeing things. So, the separation between a belief system (the past) and what follows (the present) is clear and there is nothing in the middle between the two just as there is nothing between two successive frames of a motion picture film. Their sequence is interpreted as movement, but in reality, they are two static images.

We should remember this fact because it will serve to clarify some famous linguistic paradoxes, since language reproduces our beliefs as thoughts, and as statements if we are to make them public.

6) THE FUNCTION OF FORMALISED LANGUAGE

Basically, natural language develops a system of individual beliefs and remodels them based on their individual experience. Although it is possible to transmit technical knowledge, it is almost impossible to convey the fundamental existential knowledge you acquire with experience. From the point of view of the species it is providential because every new generation is generously willing to take risks and commit those early mistakes of youth that sometimes open up new paths and are in any case a source of experiences.

It is true that individual belief systems, through transactions and compromises, become collective beliefs and behaviour, the providential "common sense" without which politicians would not enjoy lasting and often undeserved acquiescence, industrialists a predictable market, and sociologists a university chair.

Poignant artistic events and bold scientific hypotheses lower themselves to that maximum of cognitive entropy that is common sense.

But there is a minority that is reviving their own language as well as the common language.

At one point, a language had to be formed that was independent of both the subject and the context and that would highlight the correct way of reasoning. A language that could be applicable in various ways because it was without content.

This raises a question: are we looking for the roots of natural rationality, or the seeds of a more effective rationality?

Later on, I will argue that natural rationality, embodied in natural language, is still not well understood and has a surprising depth of which you must be aware before proceeding.

The search for correct rationality began systematically with Aristotle (Greece, Fourth Century BC) and continues to this day, but as an end point, we could consider *Principia Mathematica* (1910) by Alfred North Whitehead and Bertrand Russell, which identified the foundations of formalised language as follows:

a) Two key operators: negation (¬) and disjunction (∨);
b) Five axioms (propositions continuously accepted as true);
c) Two rules of deduction, that is, the transformation of the axioms: substitution and detachment.

With these simple tools you can develop axiomatic-deductive systems using the special axioms of the systems to be developed; some of these are the well-known *Set Theory* (in particular one called "ZF" referring to the names of the mathematicians, Zermelo and Fraenkel, who formalised it in the 1920s), *Peano Arithmetic* (the name of the mathematician who formalised it in 1889), and *Geometry, Probability Theory* (axiomatised by Kolmogorov in 1933).

We should note that formalised language is totally abstract (of no significance), formal, and syntactic (it only exists as linguistic symbols with rules of transformation).

Formalised language, then, is an axiomatic-deductive system that is used to develop special axiomatic-deductive systems, which are themselves abstract, but less so. In fact, they have natural interpretations: For example, *probability theory* deals with events, although not specified until the time it is interpreted in a model that is applied to concrete events.

We should note that in this abstract world, the *model* is a concrete interpretation and therefore the word *model* has different meaning from the one commonly used.

7) LINGUISTIC PARADOXES

A brilliant British mathematician, Frank Ramsey, who died in 1939 at the age of only 26, became interested in the paradoxes that had distressed and fascinated scholars of languages and he divided them into semantic paradoxes and set-theoretic paradoxes.

The first concern the truth value of statements, the latter concern the definition of special sets.

Semantic paradoxes have a father, the Cretan, Epimenides, who in the early days of classical Greece (Seventh Century BC) had this to say: "All Cretans lie". This phrase already seemed peculiar since it could be true only if it were false. Epimenides was in fact Cretan, and therefore, as a liar, he could say only false sentences.

A short remark: paradoxes are always artificial and researching them may seem futile; actually, paradoxes are useful because they allow us to study natural rationality and the human mind.

The paradox schema called *the liar* has been examined for thousands of years (!), and there is a vast literature on the subject. I myself wrote about it (Lario Sinigaglia, *La Negazione*, Tricase (Lecce), Youcanprint, 2013; *The Negation,* English translation, Tricase (Lecce), Youcanprint, 2015).

Alfred Tarski (1902-1983) believed that *the liar* paradox could not in any way be solved in ordinary language as it contains the *truth predicate*, that is, with natural language it is possible to tell the truth/falsity of each statement. The proposed solution, valid only for formalised language, is to place the *truth predicate* in a metalanguage, equally formalised, where it is not possible to generate paradoxes. Metalanguage is a second language that speaks of the first language.

However, even metalanguage is subject to the same kind of paradox if you use the *truth predicate* about their statements. It's then necessary to resort to a meta-metalanguage, a third language, in order to isolate the truth predicates spoken in respect to the second language.

And since the paradox may recur in the third language, in the end, the proposed solution is a potentially infinite hierarchy of languages, in each of which the paradox is transferred while waiting to find one where the issues of truth/falsity do not occur and there are not semantic problems.

This unsatisfactory solution is curiously similar to that of the great problems of life that are never resolved but sometimes fade away.

But is it true that the *liar* paradox is connected without remedy to natural language?

We saw earlier that every experience of the subject involves the falsification of a belief and that belief which is first considered to be true is deemed to be false by the subject, which abandons one belief system and adopts a new one.

In this way there is an update of the subject which acquires a new belief system and retains a memory of the former. The new belief system is therefore a metasystem in respect to the previous one and the subsequent language is a metalanguage in respect to the previous.

In other words, natural language automatically generates metalanguages without contradictions because they are used as metasubjects.

A sentence such as:

- *This sentence is false* - (which if true is false, and if it is false is true, then he is a *liar* like Epimenides)

cannot be said by anyone because as a present statement, it comes from a current belief therefore held to be true, but it is false, so it is a former belief.

One could say that this sentence could be stated in the time of moving from one belief system to the next, but such a time simply does not exist, just as there are no images between two successive frames of a motion picture film.

Therefore, in natural language, this sentence cannot be defined as either true or false, but it is simply meaningless, which in reality no one can confirm.

We should note that this statement for the *truth/falsity predicate* has meaning in all cases in which a statement refers to an earlier statement by changing its meaning in some way.

Set-theoretic paradoxes: in this case, the issue is more complex and will have to be clarified in two stages: the immediate result and then dealing with *set theory*.

The problem arises because there are aggregates that cannot be captured by a description because one or more elements will remain external and therefore, in my opinion, are not *sets*: the problem arises when you want to treat these aggregates as if they were sets, which they are not.

In my previous writings, I have called these aggregates "Ur", which stands for *"Universi relativi ad una proprietà"* (Universes relative to a property) (Lario Sinigaglia, *L'insieme vuoto ∅: la mente* (The empty set ∅: the mind), Armando Editore, Rome 2012).

The first and most famous of these aggregates was identified by the laborious mind of Bertrand Russell, who shared it with Gottlob Frege (1848-1925) causing considerable discomfort because it was going to spoil his theoretical construction, the first real formalisation of language. In general, contemporary scholars did not understand his genius.

The set of all sets that do not contain themselves, according to Russell, does not contain itself and therefore does not contain all sets that do not contain themselves (against its own definition).

The reader should not lose patience for the artificiality of the preceding sentence as its importance will be understood later.

"A set is a joining into a single whole of objects which are clearly distinguishable by our intuition or thought. The said objects are called *elements of the set*".

This is the definition of sets given by Cantor (1845-1918), the brilliant mathematician who laid the foundations of *set theory* and had insights of staggering depth: he discovered that infinites are not all equal (equipotent); this idea had and will have great influence on further developments of logical and mathematical thinking.

We shall return to this subject, but for now we should note that the *set* is a very normal thought such as *the apples in the fruit bowl* or *the pupils in the class*. To identify the elements of the set, it is possible to propose a rule to identify them or list them as *odd numbers greater than zero and less than ten* or 1, 3, 5, 7, 9.

We can see that sets that do not contain themselves are normal (in fact, the *set of pupils in the class* is not a pupil in the class), while those that contain themselves have a pathological nature and are not allowed as a special axiom of formalised set theory better known as "ZF", which refers to the names of the mathematicians Zermelo and Fraenkel.

So, Russell's discovery, which was terrible for Frege, was that the description of a set (called *intension*) sometimes fails to capture all the elements of the described set (called *extension*).

Russell identified the problem in the self-reference of the definition of certain sets, i.e. in the fact that the definition builds a framework to capture the elements of the set, from which the same definition keeps them out.

The mythical sinner, Sisyphus, understood the problem well since he was condemned to push boulders to the top of a hill which rolled downhill exactly because he was pushing them up.

The solution to the problem proposed by Russell was *type theory,* which stratifies language in levels so that every statement refers to lower-level objects and it is thus impossible to refer back to the statement.

The levels of language are potentially infinite and lock language in a cage of immense artificiality, which prohibits a large number of statements that do not create any paradox.

One wonders then if natural language is affected by the problem that *type theory* claims to resolve?

We can first note that the problem affects only "totalities" and not even all of them, only the unconditional ones like Russell's set.

We look at what the nature of these is all with an easy example.

Our *reference set* involves three brothers: Alfio, Bruno, and Carlo, whose surname is Tria, represented as {a, b, c}, from the moment that the sets are designated by placing the items in braces.

In how many ways can we break down the reference set? The following that result in *subsets*:

a) with three elements: {a, b, c}: in fact, the reference set is also a subset of itself.
b) with two elements: {a, b}, {a, c}, {b, c}. The order does not matter and therefore {a, b} is equal to {b, a}.
c) with one element {a}, {b}, {c}. They are sets even if they have only one element.
d) with no element {ø}, which is called an *empty set*.

What is the meaning of an empty set? It is quite simple: if I go to the home of the three brothers and I look for them, since they're out, their old aunt says, "there is no one". Therefore, the empty set indicates the absence of any element of the reference set and is an abbreviation of {øa, øb øc}. If we call the reference set "T", the initial of Tria (we use a capital letter for the name of the set, lowercase for the name of the elements), then the empty set can be called "øT". We can see that it is not true that there is no one at home because the aunt is there as well as the parents of the three brothers, but there is none of those who I am looking for and therefore no element of the reference set. From this point of view, the empty set is not absolutely empty because it contains three specific absences, those of the people I am looking for.

So, how many subsets does our reference set have? There is one with three elements, three with two, three with one and one without any element, therefore eight in total.

We can see that the *set of all subsets of the reference set* cannot be a set, and therefore we define it as an "aggregate", because it is affected by a contradiction: "T" and "øT" cannot coexist in the same set similarly to the fact that the Tria brothers cannot be absent and simultaneously present in the house.

This aggregate is precisely "UrT", that is, the Universe relative to the property of *being the Tria brothers* referring to the brothers in question, which makes them elements in the reference set.

The UrT aggregate has eight elements and the formula for calculating the number of elements of any Ur is 2^n, where the exponent "n" represents the number of elements in the reference set which, in our case, are three, i.e. {a, b, c}, therefore the number of UrT elements is two to the third power, that is, eight, as we have already noted.

The *Diagonal Theorem* by Cantor shows that the number of elements of a Ur is always greater than the number of elements in the reference set; a trivial conclusion if the number of elements of the reference set is finite but a fundamental one if it is infinite.

In this case, it can be said that the reference set has the power (numerosity) of *countably infinite sets*, because you can count the items with natural numbers, those of our elementary arithmetic, while the number of Ur items has the power of *uncountably infinite sets*, that is, intuitively so many more that natural numbers are not enough to count them.

Let's go back to our natural language and see in what precise way it can be freed from Russell's *type theory* without creating paradoxes.

A rule that everyone follows without knowing it happens when the subject of a sentence is predicated by a property, the subject is an individual or a set while the predicate is a Ur: in fact, each property indicates the relative universe which bears its name.

I said "indicates" not "captures" because the Ur aggregate cannot be captured by a definition because it does not have an *extension* since it is contradictory. In other words, a property exists only as a predicate of individuals or sets, but in itself is not detectable.

The Ur are only those unconditional totalities that cannot be placed as the subject of a sentence while it is entirely legitimate to include a conditional totality as the subject of a sentence, such as "all the pupils in a given class" or "all the citizens of Milan", which are normal sets.

Now you need to ask yourself two questions:

a) How does natural language automatically avoid the subject of a statement from being an unconditional totality? (Since this is not a grammatical rule but it is a law of natural language, i.e. the natural rationality of which we are not even aware).
b) What distinguishes a Ur from a set? (So far, we have said that only an unconditional totality – a Ur – cannot be captured by a description).

With regard to point a), the criticality occurs when the subject of a sentence is a homonym (same name) of a property: in this case, the subject is a *concept* (the extension of which is a set) and not a *property*. It is now a question of distinguishing between concept and property: the property can be denied while the concept cannot be denied and is conditioned by its own predicate or <u>by the context in which the statement is made</u>.

We must never forget that statements of natural language cannot be separated from the one who states them and their belief system, nor from the circumstances in which they are made (these are the context), and it is the very fact that formalised language is deprived of the context which determines the paradoxes.

This, however, is not critical to formalised language, which is indispensable for the uses for which it is intended, inter alia, to program a machine, but only finding that the paradox is the other side of the coin and not resolvable, as the attempted solutions already examined amply demonstrate and which are just artificial palliatives.

Let's look at a few examples of critical statements in which the name of a property figures as the subject.

a) "Humans are always human". The sentence is not a trivial tautology which states the identity between subject and predicate, but the circumstance in which it is made helps us to understand what kind of person is being talked about; <u>great or miserable</u> in this particular circumstance while in the predicate he is always <u>great and miserable</u>.

b) "Sometimes humans are not human". The sentence does not mean that the subject is an animal, but it is a person with some bestial features. The context will clarify.

c) "You are so human!" Fantozzi said this when he was humiliated but meant inhuman or nonhuman; in any case, inhuman can only be sensibly said of a person.

d) "This red is brilliant". The sentence is not about the colour red in general, but of a particular application of colour found in the context. In fact, the *red-property* may well be opaque and, in general, properties do not have properties because they cannot be the subject of a predicate.

A clarification: I wrote that the concept, as a subject, cannot be negated (unlike predicated properties that can be). Sometimes language is twisted to achieve a particular meaning and it speaks of the "undead" (who are not the living, but vampires): therefore, a concept does not negate itself (the dead) but, indeed, a new one, vampires, is created.

Additionally, sometimes the property captures the subject <u>even if it is negated</u>: this is surprising and we'll come back to this (see examples b and c).

Dear reader, the distinction between concepts (whose extension is a set) and properties (the meaning of which is a Ur) is critical to the understanding of natural language, so I invite you to produce your own examples and if you find one that contrasts with what has been said, I ask that you share it with me, as Russell venomously did with Frege (if I dare make the comparison).

Of course, it is impossible to impede particular users of language, such as Russell and other scholars who are eager to find the flaws of language, from putting an *unconditioned totality* as the subject of a statement: natural language cannot defend itself and then reacts by producing a paradox. The latter is not a fault of language but an advantage: it averts us that a misuse of the language has been made.

One last point: if the subject of a statement is a previous statement, whose meaning is changed, it falls in the field of *semantic paradoxes*, which were previously reviewed.

8) SET THEORY

I apologise to the reader since in this chapter I will give some basic notes about set theory because I want to highlight the difference between the well-known "ZF" set theory and the other one used in the previous chapter that I have named "Inat" (natural set – *insieme naturale* in Italian) because, in my opinion, it is one that uses natural language.

It is therefore once again a question of divergence between natural rationality and the one subsequently evolved.

The topic is discussed in detail in my aforementioned book, *L'insieme vuoto ø: la mente* (The empty set ø: the mind), which readers who are eager to better understand this chapter may wish to consult.

In "ZF", the empty set "ø" plays a vital role because it is the summit upon which the entire theory sits. In fact, the first non-empty set contains nothing more than the empty set {ø}.

Therefore, the empty set exists absolutely by virtue of the apposite axiom and does not contain nor can it contain any element.

Instead, with Inat, the empty set is not absolutely empty but only devoid of all the elements contained in the reference set. It therefore contains very precise shortcomings: those of the elements of the reference set and therefore it is not *absolutely empty* but *relatively empty*.

This is its derivation from natural language, in which we do not speak of absolute emptiness, but always relative absences.

"The container is empty (of whatever it should contain: biscuits or chocolates)". "There is no one in the bar (of those we are looking for)". "Nothing happened today (important, of what we want or fear, of what we expect, different than usual)".

In "ZF", the empty set is unique while in Inat the empty sets are as many as the reference sets and therefore infinite.

Basically, in "ZF" the sets with elements are derived from empty sets, while in Inat the opposite occurs because the emptiness is deducted from the full set on the basis of a fundamental axiom of language: what is there may not be there.

With regards to the significant difference, it is found in the *power set* of ZF, the existence of which is guaranteed by a specific axiom, which is the *set of all subsets of the reference set* and which contains the empty set since in ZF the empty set is a subset of every set.

The power set of ZF contains the same elements as the Ur aggregate described and constructed in chapter 7 in the "set-theoretic paradoxes", however, the Ur is not a set because it is affected by the contradiction described there, which is the presence and absence of the same set: T (reference set) and øT (empty set).

The Ur are precisely the unconditioned totality that may appear only as a predicate in language, while the subjects of statements may be individuals or sets that inevitably belong to the property which is predicated, with no possibility of generating paradoxes.

Surprisingly, in some cases they belong there even if the property is negated.

"A scream that is not human" certainly does not indicate animal origin but rather an unprecedented and unexpected human manifestation, human and nonhuman at the same time.

"An aircraft that is not human" is instead controlled by aliens who, as we know, are humanoid at best.

How do internal negatives distinguish themselves from those external to the predicate? Sometimes it is understood from the context, other times the person who states the sentence makes an arbitrary choice that will be understood later.

The issue is not simple and once again I have to refer to my previously mentioned book, *La negazione* (The Negation), where I make the distinction between *endoceptual negations and esoconceptual negations*.

9) ARITHMETIC

Set theory, in practice, is only used by certain mathematicians, those dealing with the foundation of mathematics, and the thing is curious for two reasons:

a) because it is strange that a theory of extraordinary generality serves "only" as the foundation of mathematics and;
b) because it is believed that mathematics should have a foundation external to itself.

With regards to the first point, set theory is certainly the basis of natural reasoning: I observe just in passing that the algebra of sets and the algebra of propositions are isomorphic (a Greek word meaning "same form"): they are both Boolean algebras that, perhaps unconsciously, we use for searches on databases.

With regards to the second point, natural numbers of our elementary arithmetic have origins in the *axiom of infinity* of ZF set theory which generate ordered sets, which we will call numbers, with this successor rule:

$$S_x = X \cup \{X\} = \{X, \{X\}\};$$

"S_x" means "successor" of set X, "U" is the set-theoretical operator "union", which from two sets obtains just one with the elements of both united, and "X" is a generic set.

The formula translated into English as "set-theoretical metalanguage", means that "the successor of any set is obtained by joining the same set with the set whose element is the set itself".

It that clear? No! In fact, it is for this very reason that formulas are used, which, with a little study, any reader wishing to understand them can grasp.

This procedure is for creating the ordered sets that are then referred to as numbers and are the foundation of arithmetic.

But why such a complex procedure? It should be understood that numbers, that we use to create order, are themselves an order because every natural number has a very specific place in numerical sequencing, given that between the elements there is a relationship of "greater than the predecessor" and "lesser than the successor" (<).

But, given that in set theory:

$$X \cup X = X$$

and that X is the extension of an intension, that is, the meaning of a property and not the measure of a quantity, in order to create "n" amounts of different elements these must be distinguishable from each other, while X and X are not.

Therefore, the complex construction of the above (let us remember: this is the *axiom of infinity*) has the aim to create "n" amounts of distinguishable elements, but which are also objectively ordered, since they will then be called numbers.

Can you believe that man acquired numbers this way? Not me.

Meanwhile, I note that since in general:

$$\varnothing \cup X = X; \text{ and in particular } \varnothing \cup \{\varnothing\} = \{\varnothing\}$$

(not because they are the same, but because the empty set has no element to be added to those of X or any non-empty set) it follows that, by applying the *successor rule,* ∅ remains excluded from the infinite set that the *axiom of infinity* lets you construct and therefore you cannot give it the name *zero* to which it is entitled. We must therefore insert ∅ with an unsatisfactory exception to the *successor rule*.

I also consider that the numerical series arises from an innate and ancient ability of higher animals to order the sets in accordance with quantity. After all, a squirrel unable to understand the difference between two and four nuts would have serious problems of survival.

Therefore, what leads us to numerical series is an abstraction rather than a construction.

Let's review *the aggregate of all the subsets* of the reference set examined in chapter 7 and let us remember the definition of a set: *a set is a joining into a single whole of objects which are clearly distinguishable by our intuition or thought.*

Now let's imagine a set composed of three bottles of vintage sparkling wine of the same brand and vintage that can only be distinguished by the serial numbers that are 1, 2, 3, so our set is {1, 2, 3}. Now let us construct all the subsets with the modalities illustrated in chapter 7 and we will get eight subsets: one containing three bottles, three containing two bottles, three containing one bottle, and one containing zero bottles.

The eight subsets are all different from each other, but if we abstract from bottle serial numbers, i.e. if we agree that the difference is irrelevant, taking into account that the bottles are of equivalent quality, then the sets differ only in the quantity of their elements and become sortable by quantity. It is a matter of giving a name to each position of the order and we get natural ordinal numbers.

We should note that the ZF set theory does not allow an abstraction of this kind and therefore, now being the elements of indistinguishable sets, there would only be two sets: ø and {1}.

But language continuously performs abstractions of this kind and the near totality of entries in a dictionary is an example: one can speak of "water lilies" only by abstracting from individual differences.

What do we conclude?

The ZF set theory is strikingly elegant and concise, especially thanks to the decision to postulate an empty set as an absolutely empty, unique, subset of each set, and it makes it possible to construct the set of natural numbers in a very ingenious way.

However, natural language seems to be based on a different set theory, in which the empty set is only relatively empty and only appears in Ur, which are not sets and have the meaning (so to speak) of any predicate that contains a quality.

The numerical set, as ingeniously and elegantly derived from ZF theory as it is, seems to have a different psychological foundation and is enormously widespread in the animal world because it gives clear advantages in the fight for survival. In this sense, it is fully justified in itself.

10) CONCLUSION

If I have convinced you that the language of each of us is ourselves, we should take care of it and nurture it as our most precious cultivation. It is also the voice of those who came before us, which is older than anything archaeologists could ever unearth.

Lario Sinigaglia

Youcanprint

Printed in July 2019

www.ingramcontent.com/pod-product-compliance
Lightning Source LLC
Chambersburg PA
CBHW020444030426
42337CB00014B/1385